THE BROKEN HEART TOOLKIT

P. A. THORN

The Broken Heart Toolkit

Copyright © 2017 P. A. Thorn

ISBN-10: 154312710X
ISBN-13: 978-1543127102

"Two little dickie birds sitting on a wall..."
English Nursery Rhyme

CONTENTS

ACKNOWLEDGMENTS

I wish to express my sincere thanks to Mark King for yet another great book cover and to Bryony Weaver for her superb editing skills. I'd also like to thank Rob Maynard and Terry White for their unswerving support, their friendship and belief in me.

INTRODUCTION

If you're reading this book, chances are you're in a painful part of your life. If you're at the end of a relationship then the good news is that your pain holds the key to start to heal your broken heart. I understand from personal experience how it might feel right now – that nothing will ever change, but I can assure you that things do change and will with time.

No-one likes to be in pain. Certainly, no-one likes to be in emotional pain. It's the kind of pain that seems to permeate every cell of our being and penetrates to our very core. It feels like it's become an intrinsic part of us, as if it will never leave. Is the only thing that could possibly take away our pain to be back with the person who has broken our heart? Do we wish we could turn back the clock? Just maybe, if something hadn't happened, if someone had behaved differently, could things have been different? Until someone invents a time machine then we must accept we cannot change things that have already happened, but we do however have choices we can make for our ever-evolving future.

This book's focus is on the things we can do something about rather than the things we can't. Its ultimate purpose is to help you make choices for a healthier relationship with yourself and others in the future.

My name is Paul Thorn and I'm the author of several self-help books. This book, in part, originated as an eBook published in 2004 called *When Love has Gone: Coping with Obsession*. I wrote it after a very painful episode in my life. I'd fallen completely head-over-heels for someone, but it turned out to be the age-old story of unrequited love. I don't think I will ever forget the hopelessness, anger and emotional pain I experienced back then. I couldn't understand how, or why, I crumbled into the pitiful wreck I became. It felt as though I had been destroyed. I wanted to die. How could my life, my sense of self, have fallen apart so quickly? Like an imploding star.

I question now if it ever was real love. Today, in retrospect, maybe it wasn't? Whatever it was, I do know now that I made my own happiness dependent on another person. It was a great gamble of the heart and I lost. The price I paid was high.

I spent some time in therapy in an attempt to understand what had happened to me, and to try and heal. What became apparent during these sessions was that I'd lost sight and sense of myself. It became clear to me that I had to cultivate my own emotional independence that wasn't dependent on the behavior of anyone else. I needed a new and more entire sense of self. In time I did achieve this; it was a long haul, but eventually I was able to move on with my life and since then I've had healthier, happier and more equal loving relationships with others.

When I wrote the first incarnation of this book it was my intention to share what I'd learnt with others who were experiencing the same painful, emotional condition that some might call a broken heart. Some years and indeed books have passed since the first version was available online. After a couple of years I retired the eBook, and metaphorically speaking it's been 'collecting dust' ever since. Just over a year before writing *The Broken Heart Toolkit* I wrote a book on a completely different subject which went into some detail of a methodology I'd developed over the years to find a better sense of self in the face of illness. I realized that there was a correlation between this newer book and the old manuscript I'd written some years earlier. I decided to revisit *When Love has Gone* and the evidence was quickly apparent to me – the methodology sat well in both books. So, I set to work reworking both texts to expand on the ideas I originally presented over a decade before, and to create a whole new book that not only explains the 'mechanics' of a broken heart, but also provides some tools and a method by which to work towards greater emotional independence. You're now holding the result.

The 'broken hearts' market (yes, there is such thing!) is saturated with self-help books that promise to 'mend' your broken heart. If only it were that easy! Personally, I think that such claims are unfair to make to any reader. There's no sticking-plaster solution for such emotional pain. I also believe that when we're in pain, be it physical or emotional, it's our body, or inner self, telling us that something is wrong and needs addressing. Books which offer the promise of 'mending' a broken heart (in my opinion), carry no more weight than trashy magazine features that promise to get you 'beach fit' or give you a six-pack in as many weeks. This book makes no such promises, but it does presents some tools that when used proactively will help you chart a course through stormy emotional seas as Time, the great healer, does her work.

I sincerely hope that you find *The Broken Heart Toolkit* useful on your journey, as you rediscover a new sense of who you are and prepare to learn to love yourself before you yearn to love another again.

Paul Thorn, 2017

PART ONE

1: WHY DOES IT HURT SO BAD?

We are like snowflakes, individually different to each other, and the same can be said of our relationships. Yet, like the little girl who watches from her bedroom window with wonder and excitement as the snowflakes fall to the ground in their billions, every flake appears to be the same. But as every kid is taught at school, every snowflake is unique. It's only on closer inspection under the microscope that we see this, and yet we also learn that snowflakes form in the same way, governed in their commonality by the natural laws of physics.

Like trying to describe every individual snowflake, it wouldn't be possible to describe every human relationship in a book. The author would have long turned to dust before they could even scratch the surface! It's simplistic to suggest, given the complexity of us and our relationships, that any one book alone can be the solution to a broken heart. It can, however, like a map or a compass, provide the reader on life's journey with the knowledge and tools needed to find the way from a dark place to the light. The decision on which direction to take, however, is up to the traveler.

The primary aim of this book is to help the reader build a stronger and more resilient sense of emotional independence. Many of us have 'merged' on a very deep level with the object of our affections and feel lost when a relationship ends. The natural law – the 'physics', or as I like to call it, "the mechanics" – of a broken heart works very similarly, in principle, to that of an **addiction**; we are 'bound or devoted' to something or someone, and a real or imagined need is not being met. This in turn causes us to go into a state of emotional **withdrawal**. And it's a painful state to exist in. It can cause us to act in harmful and damaging ways, both to ourselves and others **(obsession)**... but I'll talk more about that later in this chapter. I just wanted to get this simple concept across from the beginning of the book, as it forms the intrinsic foundation of it.

What is it that makes us feel that we cannot live without a certain somebody in our lives? Again, we're all unique individuals. For some of us, it comes down to the fact that something was missing in our lives when we were children. Love and nurturing for a child is a strong need, yet sadly many of us didn't get what we needed, and it can lead to problems in later life. Many of us decided that when we were old enough we would find someone who could give us the love that we seemed to lack for ourselves. If someone could give us this, and just love us, wouldn't everything be OK? Wouldn't the emptiness, the void inside finally be satisfied?

Maybe we're attracted to people who aren't going to be there for us or we're drawn to people who are unavailable (physically and emotionally), who fear intimacy, avoid emotional entanglements or have a fear of being smothered and engulfed by another person? Inevitably, for people with these traits it leads to yet another abandonment, and an ongoing quest to find 'the one' – you know, *'The One'*.

Of course, not everyone's emotional issues have their roots in childhood. We may have had an idyllic childhood, receiving all of the love, care, kindness and nurturing that every kid deserves. We may honestly be able to say to ourselves that our upbringing hasn't contributed to our unhappiness whatever. Yet, what many with a broken heart do have in common is that they've invested most of themselves and their happiness in another person. Their emotional wellbeing comes from an external source, as opposed to coming from a place within. If, as many of us do, we feel a void inside of ourselves we sometimes fill it with the presence of another person, or with obsessive thinking about another person and other often destructive compulsions to try to make ourselves feel better, to not experience the void, to remove ourselves from our pain and reality. However, the end result of this behavior is often only a temporary fix – we always need more! In the end, it has an adverse effect on us and others around us. Longer term, in cases where drink and drugs are involved, this behavior can potentially lead to illness and sometimes death.

When we see clearly the pattern of our behavior, we can try to do something about it. But firstly, we have to recognize it. As I've mentioned, there is no one-size-fits-all solution and our relationships are as different as we are from each other. I can, however, speak from my own experience – now, you may or may not identify but it does set the scene for describing the 'mechanics' of a broken heart which pretty much works the same for all of us when a relationship is in trouble or has ended.

I've been lucky enough to have been deeply in love with two people. The endings of both of these previous relationships were amicable separations, and, for want of a better word, "normal". Then I met "The One". I'd never felt with anyone the way I felt about this new person and although it lasted only a month and a few days (which is nothing, really. It's the kind of thing that happens in school playgrounds, and seems childish to talk of it now in terms of it being a 'real' relationship), I experienced emotional pain when it ended like I'd never felt before.

When the relationship finished, it felt as if a limb had been ripped off. I physically writhed around on my bed most nights instead of sleeping because of the deep, emotional, granite-hard core of pain that I was experiencing. I couldn't understand what was happening; I had found 'it', and then 'it' had gone. I thought I would never find 'it' again. This terrified me. It felt as though all was lost. I'd never experience love again.

My behavior, to anyone looking in from outside, must have seemed quite psychotic. I would call my love interest all the time, send texts, some declaring undying love, others that were just plain nasty. I would try anything to elicit a response, even if it was a negative one – hard to do when someone is ignoring you and not answering their cell! All I could think about was them, nothing else. I couldn't eat very much, and I lost weight. I felt sick to the pit of my stomach all the time and I would burst into tears at the slightest thing. I thought that I'd never stop feeling the way I did back then. It was as if my life was over. I couldn't accept what had happened – more than that, I'd gone from loving them to such searing hatred. If I couldn't have them, then I didn't want anyone else to, either! I started behaving in a way that I'm not proud of.

At this point I need to put into context some of the language I'm using. These words might be misunderstood, perceived negatively or may even completely revolt the reader, but being in love isn't always red roses and those of us who have had a broken heart know it. It might be difficult at first to apply these words to one's self. However, they very effectively describe the keystone concepts outlined in the next section of this chapter; The 'Mechanics' of a Broken Heart, (otherwise also termed 'The Cycle'). The words in question are; **obsession**, **addicted/addiction** and **withdrawal**. Let's now look in turn at what each literally means.

Obsession n. 1 the state of being obsessed. 2 an idea or thought that obsessed someone. [1a]

Obsess *v.* preoccupy continually or to a troubling extent. Be constantly worrying about something. [1b]

Addicted *adj.* 1 physically dependent on a particular substance. 2 *informal* devoted to a particular interest or activity: *he's addicted to computers.*

- ORIGIN C16: from the obs. *adj*: addict ***'bound or***

devoted'. [2]

Withdrawal *v.* cease to take an addictive drug. [3]

The 'Mechanics' of a Broken Heart work in a very similar way to addiction. There's no substance involved, but there's another person who becomes a '**need**', obsessive thinking about that need and the emotional pain experienced when we're cut off or deprived of the person we're 'addicted' to. The emotional withdrawal from a person can feel like going 'cold turkey', like an addict needing a drug that can't be supplied. In the following description of The 'Mechanics' of a Broken Heart it's important to fully understand the context in which the language is used. The words; **obsession**, **addicted/addiction** and **withdrawal** for most of us are unattractive and not labels that we would want to apply to ourselves, but to those who think this I point out the 16th Century definition of what an addict is; **"bound or devoted"**. Could these words be applied to you?

Approach the next section with an open mind, and half the battle could be won. There is the potential to make major progress if you get a grasp of understanding what I am about to describe.

Ask yourself honestly:

Can I identify 'The Cycle' at play within myself?

*Is the emotional pain I'm experiencing, the ache I feel inside because I'm going through **withdrawal** from another person, because I miss them and believe I **need** them?*

Do I want to break 'The Cycle'?

The 'Mechanics' of a Broken Heart ('The Cycle')

1)   Possibly there is a degree of absence of self-worth, the presence of low self-esteem, (sometimes as a result of neglect or abandonment as children, and an inability to care for one's self). This rule won't apply to everyone.

2)   We seek self-worth and validation from others. We seek someone who will look after us and fulfil our emotional needs. Our happiness is dependent on another person.

3)   Maybe we're attracted to people who aren't going to be there for us, who are unavailable in some

way and who usually have a mixture of the worse traits of our parents. The reason we do this may be to try to resolve old issues. Again, this rule will not apply to everyone.

4)   When we get even a small amount of 'love' or attention from another person, we feel worthy and validated in the absence of our own self-worth. Here we are looking EXTERNALLY for the source of our happiness.

5)   The attention and 'love' we have received becomes a **need** – we see it as a vital, intrinsic component of our emotional wellbeing, believing that the only person who can give us it is the person we are in love with.

6) We become more needy, seeking reassurance that we are loved. The person we're in a relationship with may give us cause to doubt (perhaps they've had a bad day and are 'snappy', they don't call us when they say they will etc.), or we ask if someone loves us and don't believe them when they say they do.

7)   The person who has provided us with 'love' and attention at some point – usually in the early courting stage of the relationship (or in the bedroom, even if it's only a one-night-stand, bearing in mind that some of us choose people who are not going to be there for us emotionally, who are unavailable in some way or who maybe fear intimacy themselves) – feels engulfed by our neediness and our wanting of reassurance that "everything is OK".

8)   Either the person we have connected to ('merged' with) withdraws emotionally but remains in the relationship, trying to change the level of intimacy, or they leave the relationship altogether. Alternatively, we might sabotage the relationship in the misguided belief that by doing this we have some control (motivated by fear), and that doing this won't hurt so much. We leave the other person first because it seems apparent to us that our lover wants to leave us. We do this because we think it will be less painful. Both behavior patterns, however, lead to the **withdrawal** stage, the place in 'The Cycle' that causes us to hurt so much.

9)   We go into a type of withdrawal when the person who was providing us with 'love' and attention leaves us, and we experience emotional pain. The withdrawal is like coming off of a drug and going 'cold turkey'. (Sometimes the emotional pain we experience is old pain from our childhood, and may be connected to past neglect, and/or abandonment, and/or our parents' separation, and/or their divorce, and/or the emotional absence of one or both of our parents, leading to an eventual abandonment of self.)

SO HERE'S WHERE IT GETS REALLY INTERESTING...

In our pain, we start to obsess about the person who has gone from our life. Perhaps we still have some contact with them, although it may not be very positive contact and may have taken the form of the cold shoulder, arguing or mutual abuse. To us (maybe we're attracted to emotionally unavailable people), this is intimacy of a sort – something is better than nothing, we rationalize – and we believe on some level that having this 'intimacy', even if it's negative, constitutes some sort of relationship. We still can't get enough of them; like a drug, we crave, yearn and long for them. We cling onto the slightest crumbs of hope and fantasy that they will come back to us, that they'll realize they've made a terrible mistake. Even these vain hopes are a form of delusion and denial.

Our hope often stopped us from progressing through withdrawal and getting well. Often, it was only when we realized that our love interest had started a relationship with someone else were we jolted into reality, finally letting go. We began moving through the pain with a degree of acceptance, however reluctantly. This for some is the end of 'The Cycle'. That is, acceptance. However, for others it made the pain and obsession worse. They may potentially (at worst) become the parody of the "Bunny Boiler".

10) Another sub-cycle within the main cycle can start at this stage, or at any point during the relationship when we experience withdrawal. When we obsess and fantasize it is a way of escaping from our painful feelings, a trick we play on ourselves.

Unfortunately, it usually only serves to make the pain worse for us. The obsession can turn into compulsion, and we pursue the focus of it, trying to get them to change their mind. All sorts of unattractive behavior can possibly start here!

11)   One of two things usually happens; either the focus of our obsession comes back to us (usually out of fear of what we will do to ourselves or to them!), taking us back to the beginning of 'The Cycle' and restoring our supply of 'love' and attention, or they move further away from us in every way, physically and emotionally. If it's the latter, then the withdrawal continues and the depth of it may intensify.

The danger is that theoretically we can go on like this forever, exhibiting increasingly scary and unacceptable behavior and tactics. We become desperate for the focus of our obsession to take our pain away.

12)   At this stage of 'The Cycle', even though we may not see it at the time, we DO have a choice. Either we continue feeling terrible, seeking 'love'

and attention from an EXTERNAL source, or we to try to develop an INTERNAL sense of emotional independence, enabling us to move on.

It's through the development of this aspect of self that we break 'The Cycle'. When we abandon ourselves, we are not taking responsibility for our own emotional wellbeing but we have it within our power to interrupt 'The Cycle'. But we have to choose to do this.

References

(1a/1b) p988, Concise Oxford English Dictionary, Oxford University Press, Twelfth Edition, 2011.

(2) p15, Concise Oxford English Dictionary, Oxford University Press, Twelfth Edition, 2011.

(3) p1657, Concise Oxford English Dictionary, Oxford University Press, Twelfth Edition, 2011.

2: MAKING THE CHOICE TO CHANGE

How do we create change? Firstly, by making a conscious decision to change and then by taking action to instigate change. We need to take responsibility for this change and for those choices. Let me explain from my own perspective...

For most of my life, I thought – wrongly – that I was a victim of circumstance. I thought I was a victim of chance and bad luck, of misfortune and of other people. For years I took no responsibility for what happened and it never occurred to me that I made many choices along the way. It's true that some of the things that have made me the person I am today are the result of the choices of other people, such as my parents, my classmates at school and my peers. Much of what I have learnt – my habits, my opinions, my perceptions of life – came from them. I did, however, choose to believe them, to take on as my own their morals, ethics and belief systems. Maybe I chose to believe concepts that are fundamentally wrong for me – perhaps the things that I had learnt weren't right for me at all?

However, I must take a good deal of the responsibility for the way my life, my health, my career, my finances, my home and my relationships are today. Just as the choices I've made have fashioned my life, so I can also change things NOW, in my future choices and decisions for tomorrow. I can choose for my life to continue how it is, or I can make a choice to try and change it – at the very least to be going in the general direction in which I'd like my life to be going.

There are no wrong decisions - no choice in itself is wrong – but we may find it hard to live with the outcome of a choice. It is fear, real or imagined, that may prevent us from making a choice to change something. We may prefer to stay with the familiarity of past poor choices we've made. Better the devil you know, right? Definitely not! Everything in life changes, nothing stays the same. A sequence of losses and gains has brought us to the point we find ourselves in at this particular moment in time.

It is at this point in 'The Cycle' (as described in Chapter 1) that we should try to seize our chance! It's through our own pain and withdrawal that we can change things. Here we have the choice of either seeking 'love' and attention from someone else (and so beginning again 'The Cycle') or trying to build the emotional independence that we have lacked. When we have a more resilient sense of self, we can begin to break 'The Cycle'. We stop abandoning ourselves and take responsibility for ourselves. When we are no longer so needy, the 'love' or rather validation we have often sought from others comes from within.

When we obsess about someone, we're self-harming and causing our own emotional pain. The scars it leaves go to our very core and prevent us, on a very fundamental level, from enjoying life. Why do we do this? Because it keeps us connected, even if it's in a negative way, to the focus of our obsession. It's like trying to reanimate a rotting corpse. We feel on a deep level that it's better than nothing. What can make this feel worse is seeing the focus of our obsession move on with their life, and possibly into new relationships with others. How, we ask ourselves, can they do that without, apparently, feeling what we feel? How can they be having it so easy? Did they ever care at all?

Part of obsession can be to seek out or create crisis, drama and tragedy in an attempt to connect in some way with the focus of our attention, thereby creating conditions and situations from which we need to be rescued. Thus, we try and affirm that we're worth saving despite what we truly feel about ourselves deep down. In the same way that we can seek out drama, crisis and tragedy we can also be attracted to people who are unavailable in some way because by doing so we set up the conditions for pain, and, we believe, create the intensity that we feel is needed to replay old emotional pain, like a CD on replay, in an attempt to resolve it.

It has to be said that we grow up with a pretty distorted view of what love is. We hear people sing how (amongst other things) they will climb any mountain or walk 10,000 miles for the one they love. Very nice! But look at it another way, no-one sings about picking up their partner's dirty socks off of the bedroom floor for the next decade or more. Frankly, we grow up with some unhealthy ideas about love and what it really is.

Another good example are the fairy tales we're told as kids. Snow White is rescued by her Prince (who arrives on a horse – how dashing!) with a kiss. Cinderella is saved by her Prince from the clutches of her Ugly Sisters and whisked away to a better life. REALLY? It's no wonder we hope that 'The One' will rescue us – surely then we'll live happily ever after? The End.

When we're on a quest to find 'The One', (perhaps kissing a lot of frogs in the process), we're not connected to ourselves. Once again, we're looking externally for the solution. It's no surprise that we can get ourselves into a state when the relationship goes wrong and we're all alone (again). Everyone loves a love story, but does it ever really turn out like it does in the movies? Someone has to do the dishes!

One of the things I've learnt about pain is that it's a natural process. Part of withdrawal, if we truly want to be successful in achieving freedom from obsession, is to go through the pain. It's the last thing any of us really wants to do (and probably the last thing you want to hear). When the pain comes, it comes in waves – boy, are those waves turbulent! We can feel panic-stricken and believe it's so bad we may die of a broken heart.

When we go into obsessive thinking, we're trying to fix ourselves. We do it in an attempt to minimize the pain and the reality of what is. The same goes for fantasizing; when we fantasize about the focus of our obsession coming back to us and saying that "it's all been a terrible mistake", there's a negative pay-off. The pay-off is that ultimately we have to face reality at some point. Obsession gets worse the longer we choose to stay in this state. We need to tell ourselves when it happens that there is a pay-off for this and determine not to hurt ourselves any more. In other words, we choose to stop doing it. Easily said!

When we obsess about someone, we keep it – and them – current in our minds. But that's a cruel trick, an illusion that we create to deceive ourselves. There is part of us that doesn't want the intense pain of loss to become a part of our past; it doesn't want us to move on, because then we would have to face the fact that the relationship was really over. So, by keeping it current inside us we avoid letting it go. In essence, we choose to exist in a self-created distortion of reality. When we refuse to accept our reality by obsessing, we are deluding, deceiving and being dishonest with ourselves. We can't move on until we let go.

Feeling needy can be triggered by our feelings of inability to cope with something on our own. We can easily fall into the trap of believing that our past traumas are still with us, ruling and guiding us. We can start to replay and re-experience the old pain which hasn't been dealt with, and become very dysfunctional. We start to feel like a child in an adult's body, looking for someone to support and care for us. And so 'The Cycle' continues, self-perpetuating.

However, our pain truly is the key to freedom from a broken heart. It actually serves a purpose; it tells us that something is wrong and needs attention. Before we can reach a level of acceptance about our pain, what it is and what has caused it, we need to acknowledge that it's there.

When dealing with pain I found it useful to

disengage with all people and places which seemed to trigger it or made it worse. This includes interacting with social media. How many of us have retaliated so publically, putting across our case in a quest for allies, to harm the person who has hurt us? How many of us have 'innocently' looked at someone's profile, or those connected with that person to find out what they are up to. Take a social media holiday and don't engage with it for a while. Time out! Take out the time you need for your wounds to begin to heal. Social media is a double-edged sword, so temporarily protect yourself from it.

Other activities such as listening to a particular piece of music, or watching a film can have the same effect. Listening to 'your song', the same sad album track over and over while crying to it is indulgent. It won't help one bit. It's better to sit with your pain, acknowledge it's there and that you're hurting. Most of all, be kind to yourself.

Dealing with pain that's overwhelming increases our risk of acting out in other kinds of 'fixing behavior' – whatever rings your bell - but be aware of what you're doing. Are you trying to change the way you feel with other unhealthy behavior?

Anything so we don't have to experience the pain of withdrawal, right, the aching of a broken heart? No, acknowledge the pain, don't avoid it. Do this, and you'll be taking the first steps on your way to recovery.

To ignite change and take control we need to make a conscious decision to do just that, to make a choice and then put in the effort to make that change. It's no good to only think about it – and it isn't all about putting in the footwork. It's a combination of the two. Once we make the choice to change we must nurture it.

Changing our life for something better can be achieved if we take responsibility and put the effort in, but it can sometimes take time and take longer than we're prepared to wait. It can be very easy just to stay with what's familiar and settle for second best, especially if the change that we want is a long-term goal and seems on first appearances to be out of our reach.

So, we can choose for life to continue how it is, or we can make a choice to TRY and change it – at the very least in the general direction in which we'd like our lives to be going, and to always be OPEN to new possibilities and any opportunities that may present themselves. If we are closed to change then those possibilities and opportunities will in all likelihood pass us by.

We can also choose out of fear not to make a choice, but in doing this we ARE in fact making a choice, a choice for inaction, a preference for what is familiar, however uncomfortable and unhappy our lives may be, because of what we already know.

We are a product of all the choices we've made throughout our lives. That includes the way that we behave and think, including allowing fear to dictate a choice of inaction. Taking responsibility for the past and where we find ourselves today takes humility. To look closely at your life and to admit to yourself that you are entirely or partly responsible for where you are can be ego-deflating if the place in which you find yourself isn't a good one. Yet this is the first step in any sort of change. It's a reality check, a turning point that provides us with a baseline against which to measure future progress, a launch pad where we can say to ourselves, "I *am* capable of change," and then make the **CHOICE** to

THE BROKEN HEART TOOLKIT

try to do things differently from now on...

We **CHOOSE** to have, or to find direction for ourselves. We CHOOSE to **TAKE CONTROL**, to OWN our future, and take **RESPONSIBILITY** for it.

3: FINDING EMOTIONAL INDEPENDENCE

Let me introduce you to the Karpman Drama Triangle – it could change the way you look at relationships forever! When I first came across this well-known psychological model my identification was immediate. Using this model we can usually quickly identify unhealthy relationships and understand their dynamics better and our role in them.

First described by Stephen Karpman (a student of psychology pioneer Eric Berne, author of *Games People Play*) in the late 1960s, the Karpman Drama Triangle is a psycho-social model of human interaction and is widely used in psychology and psychotherapy today. Let's summarize the Karpman Drama Triangle: there are three psychological roles that people may take in a situation which are very pertinent to emotional relationships. They are:

- A person who is treated as, or accepts the role of the **'Victim'**.
- A person (actual, or perceived by the 'Victim') who persecutes (or pressurizes) the 'Victim', called the **'Persecutor'**.
- A person who intervenes to assist or help the 'Victim' in an attempt to 'save' them. This person is called the **'Rescuer'**. The motive for rescuing may be outwardly unclear, for some kind of psychological pay-off, or stemming from a need to be needed, essentially to validate one's self, or reinforce a self-held idea.

Individuals playing out the Karpman Drama Triangle may switch roles unconsciously. The person who is obsessed with someone and experiencing withdrawal, feeling broken and helpless, may be the

Victim. They perceive the person with whom they are obsessed as the Persecutor. The perceived Persecutor, however, may be just trying to avoid the person in the 'victim' role and get on with their life. However, the Victim, in the grips of 'The Cycle', may perceive this to be persecution. The Victim may then change roles, becoming the Persecutor by doing something to harm or damage the perceived Persecutor, who then changes roles to become the Victim. Perhaps the person who has been wronged turns to their new lover for comfort, the Rescuer. Although the Triangle doesn't intrinsically need three people (it needs only two to function), it illustrates a point. The purpose of this unconscious 'dancing' around the roles of the Triangle is to get unspoken psychological demands met in a manner the participants feel is justified, without having to acknowledge any dysfunction. Being trapped in the Karpman Drama Triangle is exhausting, and unhealthy.

Essentially, I already knew subconsciously that I tended in life, by default, to always take on the role of Victim. What I didn't realize is that this sent out a signal to others who were also prone to playing this game. I would attract Rescuers mainly, sometimes Persecutors. What did I get out of this? It was affirmation for me of all the negative thoughts that I had about myself. They would tell me the very things I had 'learnt' (or had been programmed) to believe by my family, society and peers. I must take most of the responsibility for this; I made a choice, consciously or subconsciously, to enter into relationships like this, however brief or long-term they were.

The fact is that those who operate within this system are all playing a game that has a pay-off, however negative that pay-off may be. The Victim receives affirmation/ reinforcement of the way they see themselves. The Persecutor gets to feel superior – a 'blind' reaction that covers his or her own lack of self-worth; self-righteousness is their pay-off. The Victim often willingly chooses to receive this criticism, because they've heard it all before. It's familiar. For the Rescuer, the act of rescuing is their way of underpinning self-worth. They, too, may have low self-esteem. Rescuers often become Persecutors when they feel that the Victim isn't willing to be rescued. Or, if the Rescuer succeeds in pulling the

Victim temporarily out of his or her malaise, he or she may become the Persecutor to keep the Victim a Victim or push him/ her down into his/ her default belief system so that the Rescuer can rescue again.

And so **'The Cycle'** continues...

Often these relationships eventually implode on themselves. All parties get spent emotionally, and resentful towards each other. Love is not the motivation or creative force behind the Karpman Drama Triangle. If it is perceived to be, then it comes with rigid, damaging conditions – 'Play the game, or else!' For a relationship to be healthy, love must be unconditional.

The other aspect the Karpman Drama Triangle shows clearly is that we are able (if we are aware of the dynamics within a relationship) to take conscious responsibility, to make a choice about the role that we play. We can't control the other person we're emotionally involved with but we can control how we ourselves behave. Consequently, we become more responsible for our own emotional wellbeing.

As I've mentioned before, to make our happiness dependent on the responses and actions of another person is unhealthy and can lead us into 'The Cycle' (Chapter 1). When we emotionally 'merge' in part or entirely with another person, it's no wonder we're torn apart when that person withdraws from us. The way out of 'The Cycle' is not dependent on an EXTERNAL source – we need to develop an INTERNAL sense of worth and self which is emotionally independent. In other words, we stop being a Victim and/ or Persecutor in the Karpman Drama Triangle sense of the words and make the choice to become more responsible for the way we feel. We therefore remove ourselves from the machinations of the dynamics of this well-documented psychological model. We essentially step outside of it.

I can understand that this may, on first appearances, seem near-impossible. I'm wondering as I write how many readers have put their head in their hands and thought, "What the heck!" Yet, let me tell you something... the way we feel is a *perception* which comes from the way we *think*. Yeah, that's right – it's just thought itself. If we aren't in control of our thinking processes, if we have surrendered them and they are dependent on another's actions, when everything appears at first glance to be someone's or everyone else's fault, then we're never going to have any responsible, independent control of our own thoughts which manifest into our feelings. No-one else is going to feel the effects of your thoughts except you. It's your reality and it's created by you.

Emotional pain has the potential to be the touch-paper for immense personal growth if we choose to use it as such. The first step to working with this pain is acceptance of the way things are in this moment. That sounds great in principle. If only we could just accept things as they are, be grateful for what we have in our lives, and be happy with our lot – well, wouldn't life be so much easier? Holy moly, that's about as easy as the concept of letting go, detaching with love, and all the other clichés that are handed out when it comes to any discussion about broken hearts, emotional pain and the causes of it.

For many people who have had their heart broken, an 'emotional merger' has taken place at some point, at the very least for one person in the relationship. Our emotional wellbeing has become dependent on the emotional state of the other party. If they are up – we are up, if they are down – we are down. We might behave like an emotional mirror for the person we are with. Alternatively – and referring back to the Karpman Drama Triangle here – if one is up and one is down a Victim/ Rescuer dynamic could evolve. Rather than just accept that our significant other is having a bad day, it affects us on an internal level to such a degree that we attempt to change the situation. Instead of acceptance, we may try to manipulate an individual, even on a sub-conscious level, to meet our desires. This is trying to fit our own expectations to the circumstances we find ourselves in.

It is all too easy to live in a recent, but nonetheless historical dimension. We can waste much time, and, more significantly, the moment, when we dwell too much on the past. It serves no purpose replaying old scenarios from yesterday or yesteryear. Equally, projecting our thoughts into a future that hasn't happened can lead us into troubled waters. The majority of the time, things don't go exactly the way we plan. The things we plan can turn out completely different in reality. When we have expectations of people, we're setting ourselves up for a fall. Ultimately, we have to realize we have no control over them.

When our expectations of what reality should be don't tally up with what's actually happening, conflict can arise. We often believe, misguidedly that things are not as they're meant to be, which is essentially a non-acceptance of how things are, this moment in time, now. Our inability to reconcile our expectations with how we perceive things to be in any given moment can cause us to behave in a way which goes against the natural order of things.

If we're prone to over-intellectualize we run the risk of choosing the worst of worst-case scenarios and then trying to control or manipulate people or circumstances to avoid the imagined disaster. Sometimes the fear is so great we make a pre-emptive strike in anticipation of an event which is purely imagined. We can inadvertently sabotage things by creating a self-fulfilling prophecy. This is an act of manipulation and an attempt to control a person or the circumstances we find ourselves in. Once again the natural order – that is, what should arise out of what is real, not what is imagined – has not been allowed to follow its course. Fear of something that we only think might happen has led to an attempt to control the situation. When the concept of 'letting go' is generally discussed, it is the action behind acceptance and the relinquishment of trying to control other people or circumstances.

It's through surrender that, ironically, we win. When letting go of someone who means something to us, the important thing is to do it with dignity. We don't do this for the other person; acting with dignity is something we do for ourselves! It's a mark of self-respect, and there's a positive pay-off later for us in terms of our emotional independence.

4: IT IS WHAT IT IS

Acceptance of a situation or of the circumstances we find ourselves in isn't resignation. It is dignified, for it's the surrender of our dreams, desires and people that we truly let go. Through the act of surrender we can start to rebuild a more resilient sense of emotional independence. Our energies are better spent trying to change what we can, rather than trying to control the things (and people) we can't.

Going back to my own experience (whilst acknowledging we're all different); the recurring theme in my relationships – particularly my intimate relationships – on closer inspection was quickly apparent. My happiness was dependent on other people's actions, what they said and did, even what mood they were in on any given day. And that wasn't good, when I was serially getting emotionally involved with people who were addicts, alcoholics or damaged in some way or emotionally or physically unavailable. One of them wasn't even on the same continent at as me! Each time, I came out of every emotionally intense relationship feeling like I had gone through a meat grinder. I don't know how I managed to find these people half of the time, but I did. It was like I had secret radar (so secret even I didn't know I had one!) that could detect just the kind of person who wasn't going to be there for me and home in them. My perception of what a relationship was, the kind of people I was attracted to and the relationship I had with myself was unhealthy. It had to stop!

It was suggested to me that I abstained temporarily from relationships and emotional involvements with new people whilst I started to build a better relationship with myself. I was horrified! What the Kentucky Fried Chicken do you mean!? Are you *serious*? But if I was going to move on, I needed to stay out of 'The Cycle', so abstinence made sense, however much I didn't like the idea. Clearly, I needed to behave differently to how I had before, or else the result was always going to be the same. Seeking a rebound relationship to fill the void left by the previous one was just another way of avoiding the pain of withdrawal. Just like the addict who gets his next fix. It wouldn't heal my broken heart, only offer temporary relief from it aching so much.

Life isn't 'black or white'. Wouldn't it be easier if we could just accept and live with the 'grey', what is not understood or what is unresolved? Our quest for the neat and tidy resolution of all of our problems is driven by fear of not being in control. It's like constantly imagining how you would spend the money from a big Lottery win. The projection of how we would like things to be encourages us to attempt to control and manipulate people to our own desires, to try and make them fit our expectations.

Reaching acceptance takes practice. When there's something in my life that I cannot accept, I look back on situations from my past and how eventually I either came to a natural acceptance of them, or was forced to by circumstance. I remind myself that everything passes and changes. Emotions are like the weather; they aren't permanent. It's possible to wake up and feel completely different to how you did when going to bed the night before. Overnight a new 'weather front' has moved in and for the new day we perceive the world as a different place to how it was yesterday. Did the world actually change overnight, or merely the way we perceive it?

If we believe, misguidedly that things are not as they're 'meant' to be, we can move quickly back into non-acceptance of 'now', this moment in time. It's pointless rehashing in our heads the events of the past; that only waters a garden of resentments. It's the seeds we plant today that become the harvest of our futures. However, be aware that our projection, the way we dream of how we would like things to be in our future can also take us out of the moment, and cause us problems further down the line.

Let me illustrate the point. Once in a while we may meet someone special and the door to our heart opens. Our mind can take us on a journey, and we immediately slip into 'future fiction' – you know, where you've merged your Martha Stewart cookery book collection, and the U-Haul truck is at the door. We suddenly mentally leap months or years ahead of ourselves. "Choosing bedroom curtains", as I call it.

Like a movie that exists only in our own mind, we imagine our lives with this person. But as well as being the star, we're also the director, the producer, runner and every other credit in our epic. Then our co-star, in our opinion, stops following our direction. They don't read the script... and how could they? They don't have a copy and haven't rehearsed their lines. We may try to manipulate and control the person who is 'misbehaving' to meet the expectations in the script we've written. We become hurt, angry and resentful as they seem to be taking no notice of it whatever. They too are confused about what's going on and react negatively to being controlled. Et voilà! Things start to go very wrong with the relationship.

Is it possible that things could have turned out differently had we just gone with the natural order of things and let the relationship evolve naturally? If things have progressed too far we may never learn the answer to this question.

Ironically, the more we try to control, grasp and

cling onto someone, the harder things get. It's as if we go into relationships very well-meaning, acting like a Jane Austin character in a romantic costume drama, but potentially coming out the other end like Glenn Close in the movie *Fatal Attraction*, trying out recipes for rabbit. Once the relationship has imploded, if we can't emotionally move on (to use another character analogy), at the extreme we can become like Miss Haversham in the book *Great Expectations* by Charles Dickens. Jilted, still in her wedding dress, she waited into old age for her man to return, only to eventually fall into the fire.

When we see every relationship, even the failed ones, as a gift (however painful) surely we learnt something, even if it wasn't pleasant? This admittedly is often in retrospect. After a relationship ends we may feel a lot of uncomfortable feelings and they certainly don't manifest like a gift at the time. But it's OK to feel them; just because they're uncomfortable doesn't make them bad. Our feelings alone won't kill us, even though it may seem that way sometimes. The same can be said of fear itself; if we can see it as a gift and use it to positively instigate a shift in our thinking it can provide us with an opportunity to grow. It is through the act of surrender that we can embark on the withdrawal process and interrupt 'The Cycle'. It is also at this point we are in a position to make new choices and claim our emotional independence.

Surrender to the natural order of the world, to the circumstances that we find ourselves in, and acceptance of this moment in time sets us free. Like the little girl who watches the snowflakes fall until it settles; who puts on her little coat, wooly hat and gloves, she goes outside and lovingly builds a snowman. She wakes up and sees it each morning from her bedroom window and it makes her happy. Then the weather gets warmer. Unable to do anything to save him, her snowman melts into the ground. She cries at first, then finally accepts her snowman has gone. She knows deep down that one day the snow will fall again.

PART TWO

5: GOING INTO CHRYSALIS

In Part Two of this book we shall learn about some useful tools and how to use them to help build emotional independence. In Part One we learnt about the 'Mechanics' of a Broken Heart; by understanding and identifying our place within 'The Cycle' we're able to start to use the tools to interrupt it. Remember, it's through our pain that we grow, **if we choose to**.

Part One also covered the concept of choice and our potential reluctance to make one. The first part of this book also discussed the importance of emotional independence and outlined how building this aspect of self enables us to move on to a better relationship with ourselves, and to healthier relationships with others in the future.

Question: Are you done yet with your emotional pain?

I want you to do a bit of soul-searching here. As I mentioned in Chapter 2, "When we obsess about someone, we're self-harming and causing our own emotional pain. The scars it leaves go to our very core and prevent us, on a very fundamental level, from enjoying life. Why do we do this? Because it keeps us connected, even if it's in a negative way, to the focus of our obsession."

Some of us choose to remain in pain – to keep the embers glowing, so to speak. To quote Chapter 2 once more, "Our hope often stopped us from progressing through withdrawal and getting well".

Unless we make a choice to **TRY** and change, we remain a hostage to our broken heart. If you need to keep the "embers" burning then you're not ready for what I call "going into chrysalis". Good luck! If you have truly had enough of being trapped in 'The Cycle', and if you **CHOOSE** to, then you are ready.

So, what is meant by the term, "going into chrysalis"? Let me begin with what it doesn't mean; it doesn't mean we hide away or retreat to merely lick our wounds. It means we take steps to protect ourselves, to not expose ourselves to things or people that may harm the process when change is in progress. The main rule is that we don't contact the focus of our obsession. If we do, even if the outcome is a negative one, this is a fix for those who are "bound or devoted" to someone and it simply takes us back into 'The Cycle' that we're trying to interrupt and break free of.

When we go into the chrysalis stage, we're minimizing the contact we have with the person over whom our heart has broken. This means avoiding places where we may see them (if possible), avoiding asking others about their wellbeing. It also means not spying on their social media or having a conniption on it for the world to see. When we go into chrysalis, we do it not for the other person but for ourselves. We need space and time to work on our emotional independence and to allow the withdrawal process to unfold with minimal interference. If anyone enquires, you are simply taking time out for yourself.

The length of time you are in chrysalis is your choice. For myself, having made a conscious decision to do this I found it to be a very nice 'place' to be. During your time in chrysalis you will be using some tools; these will start to help you form more resilient emotional independence.

The method offered in this book is a very simple one that I've developed over the years and applied whenever I've wanted to find direction, to take control and create change in my life. You might be asking yourself, does this work? I can't say about you – only you can – but for me it has. Why? Because this was the CHOICE I made.

I'm a big fan of making lists. In fact, I have several notebooks in my bag right now. It's a source of hilarity for some of my friends to see me pull one out mid-conversation and start to make a few notes. The notebooks and other 'scribblings' I carry around serve two roles; 1) to provide a sort of roadmap for the near- and not-so-distant future; 2) to externalize, to make tangible what I'm thinking and feeling. More about this method later, but before we go into any depth on it, the reader needs to understand some fundamentals and basic concepts.

Listed below are categories that anyone should be able to break their life down into:-

"Health and Self"
"Relationships"
"Home"
"Work"
"Finances"

I list each of these in order of importance to me at this particular moment in time – by this I mean in terms of the areas of my life which need most attention. When I first started working with this method it was difficult to put things into any priority order because everything seemed to be a pressing issue and needed work! Things were a bit of a mess. It felt quite overwhelming. I suggest that you don't get too hung up on trying to get things in the exact order – but there is one exception. I think it makes sense to say that the most important aspect of anyone's life has to be their health. It should always be at the top of the list irrespective of which other areas of your life need attention. If we put relationships at the top of the pile then we aren't putting ourselves there first. We should always put ourselves first when the issues we face are those of the heart.

I find that most aspects of my life fall loosely into one of the categories. Allow me to describe briefly what each one is about here, then I'll go into more detail on working with each of the categories. Later in the book we'll be working with what's been learnt and put the method into practice.

Health and Self: The 'Health and Self' category covers a wide spectrum of things. The beauty of this category is that it is very forgiving and encapsulates many topics that are relevant to us. Not only does it cover physical, mental and emotional health, but it also covers potential addiction problems, self-esteem and self-worth issues, and the one that I like best – being kind to ourselves and having fun!

Relationships: For myself and many other people the next priority to Health and Self are the Relationships that we have. Again, this is a broader category than it first appears, because it includes every relationship we have, good or bad, positive or negative, from ourselves to partners (if you have one), to our friends, to those who could be termed as acquaintances and to those who we need to keep at arm's length for our own preservation.

Home: Everyone needs to have a home. Wherever we live, it's probable that we can improve our environment and surroundings. Obviously, that's what this category is about. What needs to be done in your home? Housework? Decorating? But there are issues at home that could be more complex – for example, living with an unbearable apartment buddy or having problems with others we share our home with. And that goes double if this person is the focus of our broken heart – that's got to be way more tricky than keeping up with the housework or painting a wall! It's still a 'Home' issue, so this is the category into which any issues related to it go.

Work: The 'Work' category is not exclusive to paid employment. I acknowledge that not everyone is going to be in full or part-time employment. Also, some may already be of retirement age. Others will not have to work in the conventional sense. However, this particular category, like the others, is also very broad. It can include any voluntary work, education or study, setting up a small business or actively looking for or making plans to get back into employment. This category applies to everyone, irrespective of whether they are in some kind of work or not. We can all work towards a goal.

Finances: Got no financial issues? I'll try not to envy you. But like so many others, the 'Finances' category is the one that I've struggled the most with. I've never been very good with money; I'm stupidly generous and sometimes accidently give away what I need. I seem to have a problem understanding the value of money and the role it plays in my life, forever paying bills and coping with debt! This category covers which bills need to be paid first, debt repayments, savings (if I have anything left) etc. At the very least, even if I don't manage to pay my bills in any given month, I do have a realistic idea of where I am financially. Although at times this has been difficult to acknowledge – and something I would prefer to ignore – it is in the spirit of responsibility and being in control. I do this not for my creditors, but for me.

I've provided here a brief definition of each of the categories. No two people are the same, so each of these categories is going to mean different things to different people. To help you identify how the categories apply to you, I propose we now look at each of the categories in more depth, to provoke some thought and consideration.

6: MORE ABOUT THE TOOLKIT

All aspects of our very different but individual lives have been categorized in the previous chapter. Their focus is on the things we can do something about and the things that we have some control over rather than the things we do not. If we have 'merged' emotionally with another person, either partially or completely, it's likely that we've neglected some parts of our lives. In very extreme cases when we've lost ourselves in someone else we may have also lost sight of ourselves entirely. This is not a healthy kind of relationship to have with anyone!

When we're emotionally invested in part or wholly in another person we aren't, if you like, in our own shoes. We're living our life in someone else's Nikes. We walk wherever they walk, not on our own life path. This isn't walking in union, together. We are not dependent on our inner resources, but on another's. When a relationship breaks down we can, metaphorically speaking, find ourselves without shoes and on our journey in bare feet.

I want to clarify at this point why I term these obvious aspects of our lives as tools. I've framed them in this way because when they're given attention independently or collectively they can effectively be used to cause an internal shift, a change in our thinking and outlook. It's by using these tools that we change our focus from another person back onto ourselves. We start to take ownership of our lives again.

Let's look in more detail at all of the tools. As I've said before, there is no one-size-fits-all, but consider each aspect as it applies to you and how you might improve it.

Health and Self: We can be our own worst enemies when we beat ourselves up, internalize it and consciously or sub-consciously turn the guns on ourselves. People can sometimes punish themselves with such thinking, or believe that they at least deserve to be punished. This skewed thinking has to be sorted out before there can be any progression into a brighter new future. Poor self-esteem and those nagging voices in the back of our heads that tell us we're not worth it are the most undermining aspect of trying to move forward. Speaking from experience, if you really can't find it in yourself to believe you're worth the kind of life you want... then fake it to make it! Tell yourself something often enough and it will become a tangible reality.

The premise is simple: if you want to build your self-esteem then do 'self-estimable' things! For example, be kind to yourself; try and eat well, treat yourself to something nice at least once a day, do seemingly insignificant but productive things at home such as cleaning out a drawer or have a yard sale of clothes you don't wear anymore. Most importantly, allow yourself time to daydream. It isn't something wrong or pointless, as our tutors would tell us in the classroom – quite the contrary, it serves a function. It is the time when on a deeper level we can find clarity about what we really want out of life.

Even if you don't think you're capable of making sweeping changes to your life, then see it as making tiny refinements and adjustments to what you already have. These refinements build up over time to become a bigger kind of change. Try and 'refine' something once a day. Big change starts with the seemingly small things we can do on a daily basis.

If you start to question why you're doing such seemingly small things then I say to you that none of us knows what's around the corner. See the small refinements you're making as being about preparing the ground to ensure that when an opportunity for a big change does come along everything is set for it to take root. It's a bit like tending to and weeding a garden; nothing good can grow on stony ground.

A high proportion of people not only have poor self-esteem, but also sometimes additional emotional and mental health problems.

Those with mental health issues have the additional burden of coping with the stigma that exists around this. It isn't always easy. Even those in the exact same situation have the potential to damage us if so inclined. We're not immune to being prejudiced ourselves and are capable of stigmatizing others too. We're potentially subject to the same kind of thinking as everyone else.

If you have mental health issues then ensure you're hooked into the appropriate services. I have learnt that I can quickly spiral downwards if I'm not feeling good about myself or feeling depressed. My mental and physical health are intrinsically linked and both require effort to maintain. Everyone's level of health and self-esteem is going to be different and fluctuate. There is no doubt that having a broken heart has brought on real mental health crises for some people, with catastrophic results. Always be willing to get outside help.

Relationships: As I've already discussed, self-esteem issues are common for many. I try and look back on my younger self with kindness and today I have a much better self-image and fiercely protect it. I have a small core group of friends who genuinely care about me.

Most people I know I'd term politely as acquaintances, but the number of people you know is not a marker of success or of how popular you are. I mean, how many of those thousands of Facebook 'friends' do you really know? There are people I have come across who it's important for me to keep at arm's length for the sake of my self-esteem. People who are toxic have a very adverse effect on me emotionally and if sustained it can eventually have an impact on my physical health. Over the years I've met some awesome people and others who were not so great. I guess that's just the melting pot of people that life is.

In Fall 2012 I wasn't very well and ended up having to take three months off work. I didn't feel like socializing, but it wasn't a completely unproductive time. It provided me with some breathing space to take stock of my life and to realize what I really wanted for my future. Such episodes of ill health can sometimes be a blessing if the time is used well. It was one of those pivotal episodes when making the choice to change seemed so much easier. One of the things I did was to take an 'audit' of my friends and the other people around me. On a practical level I found it useful to make a list with three columns. The headings were "Friends",

"Acquaintances" and "Arm's Length". Those who I definitely considered good friends went in the first column, those who were pleasant enough acquaintances went in the next, and so on. The list I ended up with was very telling and useful; I realized that I had fewer genuine friends than I originally thought, more acquaintances than I could fit on the list and a small number of completely toxic people in the third column who I needed to protect myself from.

The outcome of the exercise was that I developed a better picture of the people around me, those who cared about me, who I could be grateful for knowing and those who I needed to spend more quality time with; those I could be amiable towards, but not such an open book as to disclose too much information about myself – and those who I should have no communication with at all for the sake of protecting my self-esteem.

I have learnt that the few good friends I have are the cement that hold the building blocks of my self-esteem together. My advice? Stick with a handful of those whom you consider winners and the people that make you feel good about yourself.

You only need a few good-quality people around you for a little of the diamond dust to rub off and for the relationship to be mutually fulfilling and worthwhile for everyone.

Relating to Ourselves

If we are not comfortable in our own skins and with who we are, if we don't appreciate the health we have, or if we neglect ourselves, then can we expect to have positive and healthy relationships with others? To be clear, I don't believe that if you don't love yourself, then no-one else can love you. I've had two really beautiful relationships with people whom I met when I was at my lowest emotional ebb. Both of them carried me for a while and showed me love until I could stand up a bit better on my own and start to care about myself. I remain very grateful to them both. What I'm saying is that having the right relationship with ourselves (however much we may love someone else or they love us) has to be core to our ultimate wellbeing.

It took a long time and many mistakes before I realized that my relationship with myself was totally dysfunctional. I would want everyone to like me.

Indeed, I'd put more of my energies into trying to get the approval of people whom I really should have kept at a distance, rather than concentrating my energies on those whom I knew truly cared about me. It's bizarre to me now that I invested so much time and energy into trying to get them to like me when actually they were not very likable themselves. Why had I not concentrated my energies on myself? Eventually the penny dropped!

Relating to Others

Some people will already understand the principles I'm about to present. However, if you're like me, you may not have seen your relationships with others in the way I'm about to describe.

Imagine a pyramid with five steps to the top. Everyone we know – or don't know – fits on one of these steps. The most important, elementary principle of the pyramid is where we place certain individuals on its structure, mentally and emotionally, and how we categorize them. The individuals on whom we place the higher expectations are probably not aware of them; our expectations are really a projection of our own point of view, whether it's based on reality or what we think reality should be. We can become 'needy' when individuals don't behave the way we want them to, but neediness has an underbelly that is rarely seen. That underbelly is manipulation, and trying to get people to meet our expectations, which is a projection of the way we think things should be. It's similar to the manipulating tactics of the person who plays the Victim role in the Karpman Drama Triangle. Placing the responsibility for our emotional wellbeing so firmly in the hands of others is dangerous and can only lead to unhappiness and dysfunctional relationships.

You!

The most important relationship we can have is with ourselves. You occupy the top step of the pyramid. It sounds obvious, but when we abandon ourselves by focusing solely on others we are placing them on the top step of that pyramid. Those of us who were told as kids how selfish we were may find it difficult to imagine ourselves at the top of the pyramid. Being a late learner, I believed that I had to comply with others' demands in order to be loved. I was emotionally neglected and overly chastised, and my parents' failure to look after and nurture me left me emotionally underdeveloped by the time I was finally forced to leave home a week after my 17th birthday. By then, I had a deeply ingrained belief that I was only loveable if I pleased people and complied with their wishes. So, naturally I grew up learning to put everyone else's comfort and happiness above my own.

I spent my 20s feeling incomplete without my family, who by now had begun to disown me. Distance was showing me a different world, but even so, I spent my time trying to get them to love me and accept me, and to please them, but it was no good. As the hole inside me got bigger, so did the feeling of incompleteness. I sought a nurturing influence from other people, who were often older than me. They, I thought, gave me what I had needed but had not received from my parents. All it did, however, was lead me into often other dysfunctional relationships with equally damaged people. Repeatedly, I found myself emotionally dependent on others' actions and emotional states. Time and again I wondered why relationships hadn't worked and how I kept getting myself into the same situation. Healthy relationships never happened, but, I thought, I would never be complete without the love and approval of others, a trait I had been conditioned to learn.

Sometimes, to rebalance things we have to be purposely selfish – in the most positive way. Having the self-worth to put our own wellbeing first is going to be difficult for some, but not doing so is down to old programming and we have to choose to change. Try it – you may be surprised!

Partner

The second step below the top step of the pyramid is taken up by our partner (if you have one) and for many of us, the person in this position is also the one who may cause equally the most pain and the most joy. In the past I continually allowed inappropriate people to occupy this very important place, but – and here's the kick in the pants – it doesn't have to be filled. You wouldn't topple from the pinnacle of the pyramid if you were to remove the 'Partner' brick completely. For me, however, it used to feel imperative to my very survival to have somebody – anybody – there. I always felt that if this position was filled, then I would feel complete. How wrong this thinking is!

You need to fill this space with someone who wants to be there – and who **DESERVES** to be.

Again, let me dip into personal experience. For many years, I would try to open the doors to my heart and let in anyone who showed any interest in me. But I didn't actually believe that anyone who was emotionally or mentally 'well' or who had what I really wanted in a partner would want to be with me. I was constantly looking for someone to fill this position, and there was a sense of urgency about it. If there wasn't someone in this important position, then I thought I would die alone. Consumed by panic and lubricated with alcohol and drugs, I was that guy unable to stand still in a bar, running up and down by the end of the evening, looking for anyone who would have me. *Love me, love me, I can't love myself!* I hoped that any transient nocturnal union would blossom into *the* relationship that I felt I lacked. I would wake up next to people in unfamiliar surroundings, wondering, "Who is this person? What's your name? Where am I? What did we do last night?"

Sometimes short relationships did develop from such desperate beginnings. They would start well and I'd feel temporarily complete. The hole inside would get smaller at first, as it filled with a feeling of false satisfaction and warmth, but gradually, as I put all my energies and effort into trying to please the other person and hoping to God that they didn't stop liking me, the hole would start to get bigger again. I felt a cold void threatening to swallow me up. Consequently, I often put up with bad behavior from my partner. I was terrified of losing the relationship because it seemed infinitely preferable to being on my own. At other times, if someone was too nice to me I would wonder what the hell was wrong with them. I would make a pre-emptive strike and finish the relationship first, before they saw the light and had the chance to finish it. Whether I finished a relationship or my partner did, it led to the same thing; a feeling of being alone and incomplete.

Either way, I now know that when I'm lonely, it's because I'm missing **ME**. I also know that when I concentrate my energies on someone else, I'm not looking after myself. The people in my past life were not relationships, they were hostages. I just wanted the pain to stop and my feelings of incompleteness to end. It's insanity to just try and fit any old person into this role. The inappropriateness of their appointment to the position becomes another of those good ol' self-fulfilling prophecies. We spiral down again into relationship breakdown/ return of the feelings of incompleteness/ obsession/ looking for 'another hostage' cycle. There is such a feeling of urgency, such loneliness, that once again we grab the first interested (or non-interested) party who comes along. And so on, ad infinitum. We're never fulfilled. We remain incomplete.

If there is no-one special in your life right now for the 'partner/ second brick' position, just consider it 'situation vacant'. If someone comes along who is suitable for this position, then, great! But accept that it might not happen for a while or even ever. It's important that you get your relationship right with yourself first, and when we get this right we naturally become more attractive to other people. No, really. We also become more able to identify those who are appropriate for us. You don't have to settle for second best.

Family and Friends

When we learn to accept the choices of others we find freedom. Our happiness shouldn't be dependent on the choices and actions of others; happiness is something we allow ourselves to experience because we believe we're worth it.

They say that if you can count you friends on the fingers of one hand, then you're lucky. I've had good friends in the past, but they have come and gone. Throughout my 20s there were only a few friends with whom I hadn't had sex and I wasn't interested in making new friends. Friends were either people who hadn't made it yet into the 'partner' role, or who had already 'been there' and, for some reason, decided to stick around. They were people who I felt hadn't hurt me enough to warrant becoming an enemy. It's only been from my mid-30s that I've been able to form non-sexual relationships with other people.

I have had some very good friends. Sometimes we were separated by circumstances, such as someone moving abroad. Sometimes our lives had become so different that it caused a natural separation. Sometimes I lost friends because my expectations of them were too high, or they stopped being a friend and become more of an acquaintance. Some of us can have lots of acquaintances and few friends. People come and go in the fluidity of life, and sometimes we meet briefly and for a short time may have much in common, but then things change. How many times do we exchange cell phone numbers and addresses when we've met someone on vacation whom we have connected with, only never to see them or speak to them again? Our good intentions, which may have been real at the time, often fade once we've gotten back home. Reality strikes and life goes on. My firm friendships used to be something that I considered to be a secure zone – so strong, they would always be there. I, however, often failed to put in the energies required to maintain those friendships, which alone was enough to cause a drift or even rift.

Today, I have a few core people in my life whom I consider to be real friends. I feel I can really be honest with them and can expose my vulnerability and weaknesses. I try to maintain regular contact with them and just as I have entrusted them with confidences, so they have entrusted me with the same.

A major part of a friendship is trust, and it isn't usually given freely – it's earned over a period of time. One of the defining markers of friendship is maintaining someone's confidence. It's what friendships are usually built on. Don't abuse it, because there's a binding power that comes from sharing and keeping a secret.

Acquaintances

As I started relationships with some individuals and then over time stopped putting in the necessary 'friendship' energy – just as I wouldn't invest energy in myself – quite a few friends become acquaintances. Some disappeared into the ether, dissolving into the 'everyone else' category. It's possible that if expectations are high between friends, when they can't all be met the friendship can turn bad. Confidences we have entrusted to our friends may become common knowledge, Twitter fodder or Facebook food, if you will. Then, our former friends move into the 'arm's length' category.

Arm's Length

Once we start to look at our relationships, we become more attuned to what behavior is suitable depending on the categorization into which we put people. Personally, I've found putting people into the 'arm's length' category is most liberating. We don't have to like everyone to be liked ourselves. Often, once I had done this I became more aware of how I had behaved around these people. There was a time when whenever I met certain people I would greet them warmly, maybe even give them a hug and a kiss, yet deep down inside I squirmed, especially if I knew that the person I was hugging or kissing didn't like me – or worse, that I was doing this when actually I didn't like them. It just wouldn't sit comfortably in my gut. By doing this with them, I was being dishonest with them, and, more importantly, deluding myself. Such dishonesty to myself makes me feel uncomfortable on a very deep level. This isn't good for me, or my self-esteem.

Often, clear and strong boundaries need to be set up against people who we need to hold at arm's length, but it should always be done with dignity and politeness. It shouldn't be overtly defensive or offensive. I prefer, if I'm keeping people at a bit of a distance, not to see or socialize with them at all. Frankly, I have nothing to say to such people. If we do have the misfortune to meet them we may have to say "no". Some find this very difficult. Far too often, we say "yes" when we don't want to, so as not to displease people. If another's behavior is unacceptable to us, we must let them know it's unacceptable and that they've crossed the boundary line. Having boundaries is an act of self-worth and saying "no" to someone is setting a boundary. But like other principles discussed so far, learning how to set boundaries takes practice.

When I started to learn how to say "no" and refused to accept behavior that directly affected me, it was very strange. It certainly sorted the good from the bad in terms of who my friends were. The positive effect of practicing this principle has improved the quality of friendships that I now have and made them more enjoyable. Setting boundaries is about protecting ourselves and our self-worth; we do it for ourselves because we're worth doing it for, however uncomfortable that may be at first.

It is, however, important not to bad-mouth or

tattle-tale about people. When we do that, we're inviting them into our 'reality'. And we shouldn't allow them – or their past transgressions – to exist rent-free in our heads. We shouldn't hate them, we should detach by remembering that it's better to "live and let live"'. There's room for all sorts in this funny old world we inhabit.

Everyone Else

For good reason, this category of relationship dynamics sits on the bottom step of the pyramid. The lowest part forms the largest group. We will only ever know the smallest, passing details about these people and we'll never come across most of them more than once – on the street, at the movie theater, in the queue for the bus, so how can we also have better relationships with people whom we've never met?

Once again, it all comes down to us. Though we never speak to or acknowledge others we don't know, we can and often do make judgments about them. We may base our judgments on the way they look, the color of their skin, if they identify themselves (by the clothes that they wear or by their hairstyle) with any particular group or affiliation. Whether they look happy or angry, we figure out just by looking at someone if that person is likely to be a threat to us. In a world driven by market forces we may also judge a person by the fashion labels they're wearing and what we perceived to be the cost of their clothing. In the same way, there are many aspects of ourselves that we communicate to others without ever saying anything.

Let's revisit that saying "live and let live": how many of us practice this in our day-to-day lives? Making assumptions about others based purely on their appearance means that our perception of them is often wrong.

We're only human and our perceptions of others and the world around us is merely a projection of our own reality. Our perceptions are based on our past 'programming' and often received from a very early age. We nearly always consciously (or subconsciously) adopt the perceptions and moral philosophies of our parents, and they surely can be and are often wrong. They too are only human, so it's possible that our perceptions, which relate directly to our reality, are wrong also.

I'm not going to suggest here what's right and wrong, but I would ask you to think more seriously about what "live and let live" means. Instead of holding onto your judgments and perceptions of others, I encourage you to let them go. The only person you need be concerned about is you. And you deserve all of your energies.

When we choose not to make judgments about others we, in turn, feel less judged by them. When we don't spend our time worrying, or constantly make judgments about others we are more focused on ourselves. We can't change anyone else; the only person we can choose to change is our self. We need to accept others for what they are, whatever that may be. After all, our approval of them isn't relevant.

Home: All of us need somewhere we can live, feel safe and secure, and it should be a place where we enjoy spending time. Maybe you rent a room or apartment, or are buying or own your home? Whatever your living circumstances, the *order* in your home is a reflection of, and directly affects, your physical, emotional and mental state.

Out of all the categories presented, 'Home' is

the one where we can create a tangible impact very quickly. In terms of taking control, it may be as simple as having a good clean-up, or maybe you have grander, makeover plans for where you live? Whatever you need to do, the benefits of getting on with it should not be underestimated. Even making the smallest refinements to improve your living conditions is good for the soul. More than that, maintaining things at home is a 'self-estimable' thing to do. Again, do it for you and for no-one else.

My home used to be a mess! I felt so overwhelmed whenever I attempted any chores, to the point when I just felt like crying whenever I tried. I hated where I lived, I didn't want to spend time there and I felt ashamed of it when anyone came to visit. It wasn't a good, restful place to be in and it wasn't good for me in any respect, physically, emotionally or mentally.

Once I'd finally got a grip of myself and made the choice to take control and change things in my life, I realized that I couldn't continue in the way I had been going. Taking control at home became the first visible improvement that I achieved. It also cost virtually nothing – I'm certainly not suggesting

Property Brothers here. The benefits on an emotional level were well worth the effort that I put in, and progress was piecemeal and day by day. There was no way I could tackle the issue all at once, but collectively these small refinements turned into a bigger change.

Firstly, I had a major clear-out. I'd hoarded so much stuff over the years, terrified to let anything go (particularly documents, brochures, magazines etc., which I was unlikely ever to read). It was very cathartic and liberating to throw away what was no longer needed and start to take control. It physically felt like drawing the line between old and new ways of life. Choose to be ruthless! I would ask myself, when was the last time I used or needed the item I was considering getting rid of? If I wasn't sure, I'd next ask myself, what's the worst that could happen? In the whole scheme of things, did it really matter? So, invest in a shredder, get rid of any papers that you don't need to keep, especially old bank and credit card statements, for example, that are more than six years old. File the papers away that you're keeping – I have a file for every fiscal year – because you may need such documents, and as much as throwing a recent bill away may feel good, the debt will remain. Do the same with clothes that don't fit and other items which have become obsolete. Once you have gotten to the point when you have pared down what you are going to keep, get cleaning and make the other refinements that you can realistically do on a daily basis to improve your home.

Does all of this sounds obvious? That's because it is, but for me the degree of control that I regained in creating this new order at home makes it worth mentioning. By putting the effort in, I started quickly to feel less like a ship without a rudder.

The rule is, less is more. Home needs to be somewhere that's ordered in the chaotic world. We're bombarded by marketing that strongly suggests life should be about accumulating as much as you can. Don't be fooled! The most enlightened people often live with very few possessions. Know the difference between what you actually WANT and the things that you NEED. Once your primary needs are met, of course a little of what you want is a nice thing, but it's not the end of the world if you don't have ALL that you want. That's an ambition for another day. I will cover the subject of Needs vs

Wants shortly.

The world can be overwhelming from time to time, and home should at least be the one place that isn't. Having a sanctuary where you can sleep soundly and wake up feeling content with your surroundings is the best medication.

Work: Where does your money come from? For those who already have a job, great! Being in work is good for your health, because it provides a sense of purpose and keeps you mentally and physically active, it strengthens your self-esteem and sense of personal wellbeing. It needs to be viewed as an important part of the package of staying well and healthy.

Firstly, I know personally how difficult it can be to get back into employment if you haven't been in the workplace for a while, particularly if that means starting your career from scratch again.

You may need to get yourself into the mindset where you're fully prepared to start again if need be. Nobody in their later years wants to eat canned potatoes every day of the week and sit there worrying about how to pay the next monthly instalment on the car. This is your opportunity! What do you want for the rest of your life? What kind of work would you like to do and think you can make a go of?

Again, we find ourselves at the place where we can, if we want to, make a choice for change. This is as much about drawing a line underneath what went before and what could be in the future. And just the action of deciding, "I want to go back to work" is the first major step. That in itself will allow you to be open to new opportunities out there that you might not have been in the 'right place' to consider before. Perhaps you will need to retrain or go to community college to study, or maybe you need to do some voluntary work to get some experience? Could working for yourself be an option? Create a resumé: there are lots of different ways to write one and it doesn't have to be chronological. If big gaps are a problem, make it a competency-based resumé. Look online to find different ways you can present it. Once it's done, make a few trial applications for jobs that you like the look of and think you could do. What's the worst that can happen? Chalk up the rejections to experience and learn from the mistakes you make.

The important thing is that by putting in the effort you are at the very least making yourself available, to be open to whatever new opportunities may come along. If the door to a new future is partially ajar it's more likely to swing open than if you have made the choice to keep it firmly shut.

Finances: Previously, I've written about making the choice for change, health and self-esteem, relationships, home and work. The reason that I've placed 'Finance' as the last category is not because it is the least important; it's because there are a few other concepts that I also want to present in this chapter that will be relevant to finance, yet which are intertwined with what I've already discussed in the previous chapters. It'll all make more sense and come together before you move onto the Method. Stay with me! So, back to 'Finance'. At some point, how much money you have available comes into play. How much does making the choice for change really cost?

The answer to this question is that it doesn't have to cost you anything should you choose it not to. It's first and foremost an inside job, about how you feel about yourself and perceive the world around you. I'm not saying that money isn't important and I can tell you from personal experience that having more money than you need will not change the way you feel about yourself and life in the medium to longer term.

I received a substantial amount of money for a medical negligence case in the late 1990s. I wasn't expected to live very long when I received the compensation, so I used the cash to try and enjoy what time I thought was left. Knowing what I know now I'd certainly have done things differently! I had some 'quick-fix' fun along the way, but ultimately having money didn't make me happy. I could more or less have what I wanted – but I just didn't know what I *did* want! It was, if anything, frustrating and burst the bubble of my thinking that plenty of money would and could change the way I felt. It was an important and valuable lesson to learn, albeit a disappointing one to discover, that having plenty of money wasn't the answer.

Let me explain. There's a big difference between what we NEED and what we WANT. Our wants are going to be as many and varied as there are people in the world. More often than not, the things we think we want are not needed by us at all. We just think they would be nice to have, or, maybe at the other end of the scale, that we've "got to have them right now!"

It's taken me a long time to discover what makes me happy. As I've mentioned already, from past experience it isn't money or material things; they are merely nice to have. So long as my needs are met and a few of my simple wants, then I find that for the most part that's enough for me to be content with my lot in life: a good work-and-life balance, the money to pay my rent and not to have to worry about the next electricity bill, to be able to go out and have a drink and socialize with friends, to have a meal out a couple of times a month, to be able to buy some nice clothes occasionally, the odd weekend away and one or two holidays a year. This is what I want for my future and I don't think that it's a tall order. They're all achievable goals to have.

Sometimes when my desire to have something is very strong, I can become unsure if I actually *need* it or just *want* it. I'm reminded of a quote from the 1980s film *Wall Street*. For younger readers who haven't seen the film, it defined a decade of greed and excess. The line I'm thinking of is said by a young stock broker, Bud Fox (played by Charlie Sheen), to the greedy tycoon, Gordon Gecko (Michael Douglas). I don't remember it verbatim, but it goes something like this: "Just how many yachts can you water-ski behind at once, Gordon?" A good question! There's only so much anyone actually needs, and once we've realized that we own nothing, that we are merely custodians and trustees of the things that we have for the time being, letting go becomes easier.

Truly understanding and knowing the difference between what we need and what we want is liberating – it helps us to focus on what's really important. Our needs must always be the priority.

I've mentioned before how writing lists helps me get perspective. A notebook is an essential bit of kit. I have a page with two columns, titled "Needs" and "Wants". It helps me to discover if the "must-have" purchase is something that I could live without, even when my feelings tell me I can't. The majority of the time I come to the understanding that maybe I don't really need what I want so badly after all. This doesn't mean that I come to a state of acceptance that I shouldn't have anything. Quite the contrary; what this exercise does is put into perspective my strong desire to have something. I start to see the thing I want differently, and realize that I can't have it right now. It becomes a goal, ambition or dream for the future rather than a "must-have now" and allows me to continue to ensure that my needs – the things that are really important in order to live – are not compromised by an impulsive purchase or commitment.

Yes, a little bit of what you want does you good, but when you can afford it. If you can't have what you want today, make it a goal, ambition or dream for the future. All anyone has is today. If everything we wanted and desired were to come to us in one go, right now, then what would there be for us to aim for tomorrow?

Having the money we need is a necessity. The rent and household bills must be paid. We need to eat, we need clothes on our backs and it's very important to have some fun along the way, otherwise what's the point of it all?

Early on I got used to living for the moment. I

had a 'devil-may-care' attitude about money so that when I decided to take control there was quite a financial mess that needed to be cleared up. This has been an ongoing process that still continues today. Admittedly, I can feel resentful sometimes about my hard-earned cash seemingly evaporating from my account on the day it's paid, but the truth is, that's the reality of life, however much I don't like it.

I had to bite on the bullet and list what I owed to my creditors and also what income I had coming in. I made realistic re-payment proposals to my creditors and for the most part I manage to make those payments on the day that money comes into my checking account. It hasn't been easy, but over time my debt has decreased considerably. I can cover the cost of the things I need and I have a little disposable income each month which allows me to do and buy some of the things I want. As each individual debt is finally paid up, I'm clearing the wreckage of the past that I (yeah, me!) created piecemeal. By making a choice to address the problem I've taken control of it. If we're going to attain the kind of life we want for ourselves, then we must take responsibility for it. No-one else is going to do it for us.

Today I have only one real aim: to improve the quality of my life. I've said before about making a "refinement" to at least one thing once a day and how these refinements build up overtime to create a better standard of living. This is a daily rule that I stick to, without fail, whether the refinement is small, such as clearing out a kitchen drawer, big, like redecorating a whole room, paying a bill I resent paying or buying myself something that I really want (if I can afford it). It's these things collectively that improve the quality of my life, or what I like to call "QOL".

In the past, life has been very difficult. There was the wreckage of years of drinking and drug-taking in my younger years and a mountain of debt that had paid for the privilege. There were the hangovers and the comedowns that were so bad I couldn't go to work. Then there was waking up with people who, through a pair of beer-tinted glasses, had looked alright the night before and in the morning looked quite different. I'd roll over in bed (hoping my bed guest wasn't a 'morning' person), yet again on the edge of tears, wondering what I'd done with them the night before. I'm reluctant to call it a lifestyle because it was more of a painful existence. I had no "QOL".

QOL, for me, includes not having to do the washing up (I hate it!) so I bought a dishwasher. I hate household chores, too, so I have a cleaner who comes once every two weeks to blitz my apartment. It's £15 well spent. I throw away socks and briefs when they become worn or a hole appears and replace them, because I deserve it. I insist on having clean linen on my bed because I sleep so much better. I spend time cuddled up with my cat on the sofa and watch silly films that I've seen a hundred times already, but so what? I like them! I don't engage with people who tattle-tale, because if they're doing that about others they'll probably do it about me too. I don't have a Facebook profile for this reason. What other people think of me is none of my business. I don't answer my cell phone if I don't want to speak to the person calling right there and then. I don't have sex with people if it isn't the kind of sex I want. I allow myself to enjoy things, even if they aren't fashionable. I sing very bad karaoke and don't care what other's think. I'm doing it for myself.

I mentioned about writing a list of things that you're grateful for. Is your glass half full or half empty? What I mean is, are you a half-full or half-empty sort of person? The difference is merely the way we perceive ourselves and the world around us.

The power of gratitude never ceases to amaze me, and feeling gratitude can completely change your life for the better.

But back to the list: writing down things that you are grateful for, often just small, daily things, can cause a positive shift in the way you think and feel in a very short period of time. I've written a gratitude list regularly for nearly twenty years and in my darkest moments this simple exercise has really saved me. Mainly from myself. It's so easy to get trapped into a way of thinking that's negative. It's a personal hit job that isn't an easy mental and emotional state to live with because it taints everything, blinkering us to all that's good in our lives and to the opportunities out there.

I used to think that having more of everything would make me happy. Once I had attained whatever I'd set my heart on there was always a feeling of disappointment because any satisfaction or positive feeling gained was always short-lived. I'd then start looking for the next 'quick fix' and focus my efforts on getting it as soon as humanly possible. Having this sense of urgency about almost everything is not a good way to live. I was always chasing something, so much so that it took me away from 'the now' and my ability to live in it and enjoy the current moment. Someone very wise once asked me where my feet were. I didn't understand what I was being asked for a long time, but I realized eventually what they meant: where was I in THAT particular moment of time? Put very simply, what has passed is history and the future hasn't happened yet. Don't concern yourself too much with it. All any of us has is **NOW**.

Gratitude for what we have today costs nothing. It's really not difficult to get, either. I'm not talking about the fleeting feeling of something being nice, but really feeling gratitude deep down in your gut. Crack this, and the rewards are beyond most people's imagination. (Personally, I can imagine quite a lot!)

Here's what to do: you can write a gratitude list on anything – a napkin, if you like! I keep a dedicated notebook for mine. I used to be in a very negative place and unhappy, and at first I found it difficult to think of anything to be grateful for, so I had to keep it very simple. I wrote down the obvious: I'm alive, I have my senses, I have all my limbs, I have somewhere to live etc. Over a short period of time the list got longer and the practice of writing it stopped feeling like a chore, mainly because what I actually got from writing it was so positive. I can easily write down over fifty things in my life I can be grateful for now, and the feeling I'm left with when I come to the last items on the list is a heightened sense of satisfaction for everything I have. When we are grateful for what we already have and really feel it by acknowledging it's there, the world around us becomes a different place.

Writing a gratitude list can set you up for the day ahead and influence the way you behave, think and feel. And the most exciting thing about practicing this tool on a regular basis is that it makes you open to receive even more to be grateful for. If we can't be grateful for what we already have, then why the heck should we notice when anything else that's new and good comes to us?

7: USING THE TOOLKIT

Many of the issues that have so far been discussed in this book are relevant, poignant and common to everyone. Life isn't always easy and the added burden of a broken heart can make it more difficult – if we allow it to be. It's easy to fall into the trap of feeling (and living life) like a victim, of being negative about the future and having a sense of urgency that forces us to imagine a future for ourselves that hasn't and might not ever happen. It takes us away from 'the right now' and today. We can live with regret for the mistakes we've made or those that we blame on others, a throwback to a past that we can't undo. It helps sometimes to get a fresh perspective when we notice that our thinking has become negative.

OK, so we know a bit about the tools, let's try and apply some methodology to them. The tools described in this chapter are useful for establishing where we are right now; to recognize and acknowledge the good things that we already have in our lives, and to find direction and take control of a happier and more optimistic future. They can be used either on a daily, weekly, monthly or even yearly basis. However, I suggest that looking too far into the future isn't always a productive exercise. Life has a way of forcing us to change our best-laid plans sometimes. It's about finding what works for you in terms of frequency.

As well as writing a gratitude list every day, at least twice a week I tend to take an audit and review where I'm at. I also have an ongoing list of goals of different sizes, some small, some bigger. I try to make one small refinement a day in an effort to meet these goals. Collectively, when the fruits of these three steps come together my QOL improves tangibly and I feel happier and more content with my life. I am more emotionally independent. My

QOL relies on me putting the effort in and isn't dependent on someone else.

Some of you will disagree with (possibly be mad at) what I write over the next pages, but likewise others will instantly identify, recognizing themselves. Either way, if this chapter churns something up inside you, if it provokes some soul-searching and self-examination then maybe the point is made. What is presented isn't a magic formula for happiness; its intention is to cause a shift in thinking and to encourage people to let go of negative ideas about themselves. All of the tools presented here and the Method are designed so that we're putting our energies into ourselves and not someone else.

I should also say that it doesn't *matter* if you don't achieve what you were aiming for. It's the intent itself that's important; it allows us to be open to new opportunities and prepared for the good things that life has to offer. There is no outright failure – there can always be progress towards our goals.

Viewpoints

There are three very different mindsets/ ways of looking at things that we need to employ in this Method: 1) from the perspective of an adult/ parent; 2) that of a third person looking in; 3) and that of a child.

When reviewing our life (Step 1) we need to look at things from an 'adult' or 'parental' perspective. We need to be fearlessly honest with but always kind to ourselves. The process of reviewing our lives is not to be used as a stick to beat ourselves up with, even if that's our past experience of treatment by other adults, or indeed possibly our own parents.

In Step 2, which is about developing a sense of gratitude about what you have, the best way I find to look at this is from the perspective of a third person, someone looking from the outside in. What good things in your life could they identify?

When it comes to Step 3 and the 'making choices/ setting goals' aspect of the Method, we need almost to approach it in the same way as a child would, dreaming of what they would want for their future, with innocence and wonderment. A word of caution: it's very important that these 'adult/

parental' and 'child' viewpoints or mindsets never get to meet! By that I mean that when reviewing your life, the hurt, sadness and disappointment held by the 'child' part of us must not play a role. Likewise, when making choices of how we want to change and setting goals, the more critical viewpoint of the 'adult/ parent' must not come into it whatsoever. When these two mindsets are in play at the same time there's a possibility of emotional pain and a feeling of hopelessness. This is negative thinking and will not create the internal environment for change that you're aiming to achieve. With a bit of practice you will find it gets easier to switch between mindsets, but when you first start to practice the Method you might prefer to leave a day in between each step so you can ease yourself into the right frame of mind.

Method

For the following three practical steps all you'll need is a pad of paper, a pen and a quiet space for contemplation. I find that an A5 pad works best for me and is easy to carry around. OK, a Notebook or Mac Air may seem a better recording tool, but what if you run out of battery just when you get a great idea you want to get down? That paper pad is looking real good right now, right?

Step 1: Reviewing your Life (Adult Viewpoint)

To be sure of where things are at 'in the now', in this current moment of time we need to review our life. Most people can divide their lives into the categories I've described, so write each of these headings on a sheet of paper. Each of them needs to be considered separately. I stress again that you need to be fearless and honest with yourself, in an 'adult/ parental' mindset. Try not to let emotions govern what you are writing. Here are some things that you will need to consider for each section heading.

Take your time when considering each aspect. Beware of any sense of urgency within yourself.

Health and Self: your health is the most important thing that you can have. Without it, life can be very difficult. Write an honest appraisal of where things are at. Do you have any health issues? Are you overweight? Do you eat healthily enough?

Do you need to stop smoking, or drinking, or have other substance-misuse issues? Do you need glasses? Do your teeth need the attention of an orthodontist? Which good aspects of your health are you happy with?

How do you perceive yourself and how do you think others perceive you? Also, review other important (seemingly trivial) aspects of yourself – for example, the clothes that you wear. Take a look in your closet. Do you like what's in there? Do the clothes in it define you? Is it how you *want* to be defined? Are you unhappy with your hairstyle, (or lack of hair!)? Do you like or dislike the way you look?

Relationships: by relationships, I mean all the people in our lives. Start with the most important relationship... WITH YOURSELF! Then think about people in order. Perhaps the next person might be a significant other **(THINK!)**, or a family member. Then best friends, and finally acquaintances. I also found it useful to write down those 'arm's length' people. They may be holding us back or having a particularly negative impact on us. Next to each person's name write down what's good, or not good, about the relationship.

Home: most of us are fortunate enough to have somewhere to live, but is it the kind of home and area that you want to live in? Is your property rented, but you'd always hoped that you would have been able to buy somewhere? Is there enough room for you (and your family)? Are you happy with how it's decorated? Is it tidy or untidy? Do you not have enough to be comfortable or do you have too many things. Do you hoard? What do you like about your home, if anything? Write it down.

Work: for some of us, work is part of our lives. You may be fortunate enough to have a job, but it may not be the kind of job that you want to be doing. Do you earn enough? Do you think that you're worth more? Also, write down your achievements, things that are work-related and you are proud of. (This review exercise isn't only about things that you're unhappy with – I also acknowledge that you may love your job!) Think of it as if you were checking what food you have in the cupboard. The good stuff also needs to go down on paper in your review.

Finances: they're a fact of life, whether we like it or not. Finances need to be managed and they're more than likely also linked to our job/ career, unless we are lucky enough to have won the Lottery! So, reviewing your personal finances is very important. It is likely they're going to be central to the decision about what kind of change can be immediate and which goals are going to have to wait a while until we have resolved financially what is in hand.

Make a list of what you definitely know you have in terms of income. Do not include income that you aren't sure is definite. Next, write a thorough list of what you owe. By thorough, I mean absolutely everything! Leave nothing out. This for many this is the most frightening part of the review exercise, but remember that you're approaching this with the 'adult/ parental' mindset, so don't let the fear of the 'child' come into play. You may need to work hard to remain emotionally calm dealing with the 'Finance' category of this exercise. It terrifies me! The most important thing is that by the end of the process you have a really clear idea of where you are in terms of your finances. DO NOT GUESS figures; if need be, dig out statements, nasty letters, bills etc. AND WRITE IT ALL DOWN! Perhaps you only have limited or no financial problems? Write this down also. It is something to be grateful for.

What Next?

If you're new to the Method, I recommend not moving onto the next stage until a day or two after completing the Step 1 review. Sit with the feelings that have been generated by completing this part of your life review. It may not be comfortable, but you may be surprised about the revelations that can come up. If they're relevant, add them also to the review.

Step 2: Getting some Gratitude (Third Person)

This time I don't want you to be so 'adult/ parental' in your approach. I want you to try and look at your life through the eyes of someone who isn't you, a third person. Write a list of all of the things that you can be grateful for and use the section headings I mentioned before, if that helps. Even if you don't FEEL grateful, write down things that you COULD be grateful for. Start each item you could be grateful for with the prefix "I have...", or "I am..."

E.g.,

I have my health

I have a job

I am going on holiday soon

Get right down into even the simplest things that you COULD be grateful for (even though you may not FEEL it right now).

E.g.,

I have my eyesight

I am able to walk

I have a roof over my head

At first, you may find it difficult to think of things that you could be grateful for, but I remind you that this is an exercise, which means sometimes just going through the motions. Try setting yourself a target, for example, of ten or twenty things you

COULD be grateful for and increasing it by five every time you write a list.

It's important for this exercise that you do not just add to an old list – you need to write it every time from scratch. By externalizing the things you think you COULD be grateful for on paper, you eventually start to FEEL them. This really is a type of brain training, so I recommend that you do this on a regular basis for the best effect. I personally go through periods of time, sometimes weeks at a time, where I'm writing a gratitude list every day. And, like I said, I can say now that I enjoy writing them, because if you keeps doing this, even if it feels very mechanical at first, in time you'll start to FEEL gratitude for the good things you have in your life. It's a nice feeling, addictive even (in a good way!), and is a great way of getting perspective and an Instagram shot of your life. Keep doing the Step 2 gratitude exercise until you start to FEEL gratitude. It doesn't need to be an overwhelming feeling, but the 'green shoots' of feeling thankful. It happens quicker for some people than others. Persevere! Once it starts to happen, you'll be ready for Step 3. The fun part!

Step 3: Setting Goals (Child)

This is where the fun begins. You need to approach this exercise from the mindset of a 'child', with wonderment. Dream a little! Most importantly, don't let the critical, 'adult/ parental' part of you have a say. It will try, so push it out whenever it says, "That isn't possible, get a grip, who are you trying to kid?" etc. The two mindsets must never meet when going through these exercises. If they do, there's a risk you'll quit before you've gotten started.

Using the same headings as were used for the Step 1 exercise when you did the review, write what you would like your life to look like, how you want to feel about yourself and how you would like others to perceive you. Below are some examples of the kind of thing you may choose to change, but ultimately it's YOUR LIFE, so it is for you to write down what you want and not for me to tell you. Use my comments as a guide only. This exercise is about identifying what YOU want and setting YOUR OWN goals.

Health and Self: we would all like to be in excellent health. What could you do to improve it?

Eating healthily, going to the gym, losing some weight, working on a more defined body shape? Do you want healthy gums and pearly-white straight teeth? Do you want to give up smoking, drinking, or possibly other substances? Would you prefer to have laser eye surgery and not wear glasses anymore? Would you like to train for a marathon? Is there some prescribed medication that you need to be more regular at taking? Write down what your ideal health would be. If you're happy with the way things are presently, write that down also.

The focus on self is about inner change, not external change. You may find when you look back on the review of your life you carried out in Step 1 that a lot of it was about what you have and haven't got materially. Often these things are of concern, because deep down we worry about how other people perceive us as an individual based on what we have got, what we haven't, what we do for a living or where we live. Effectively, we think of ourselves as a kind of brand, but the reality is that changing our life goes way beyond the brand of who we are. It is about change on a very deep level – in other words, it's an 'inside job'.

Relationships: this is a term I use to cover a broad spectrum. Like I said, I mean ALL people we have interaction with, but most importantly the relationship that you have with YOURSELF!

IT IS ALL ABOUT YOU! Anyone who tells you any different is talking garbage. In each of our independent lives we are the one constant and we need to be there for ourselves. This is not a selfish action, but a necessary survival response to the world around us. The priority goal has to be that we end up feeling comfortable in the 'meat suit' we live in, comfortable in our own skins. If as kids we became used to being told we were selfish, attention-seeking and only thought of ourselves, then we can sometimes carry this crooked thinking into later life. If this is the case, then it's something that you can start to change right now, if you CHOOSE to! For the purpose of changing this perspective you will need to become what others may think of as selfish and self-centered. Once you have gotten your relationship right with yourself, you will be in a better position to give more of yourself to others. Again, do this for you and for no-one else.

Most people only have two or three really good friends, people they can call at 3am when in trouble and need help. If you have more than two or three, then count yourself very fortunate indeed! If you need to make a couple of really good friends, then what kind of people would you like to be friends with? Who do you see yourself associating with?

What about the people who you associate with today? Do they really have a place in your life? If not, then also think about letting them go. Sometimes things need to be knocked down before they can be rebuilt. Change often isn't a comfortable process: a useful analogy is that a new house can't be built on a plot of land if the old one has yet to be demolished.

Home: if you're happy with your home, then great! If not, what would you like to change about it? How would you like your home to be? Would you like it cleaner and tidier, or does it need to be redecorated? Perhaps you want to move to a completely new area or zip code and start again? If you're a hoarder or just have too much stuff, do you need to have a clear-out? Don't underestimate the power of downsizing or getting rid of clutter and re-organizing things – it's a very cathartic process. It's one of the best ways of at least giving yourself the feeling you're starting over. Having a clear-out for the most part doesn't cost anything either – hey, don't forget that yard sale! The key is to be ruthless. But if your home is just right for you, then write that down too. Another check on your gratitude checklist.

Work: would you prefer to be doing something completely different from what you're doing now? What is it that you would like to do? What's your dream job? Again, be careful not to let the 'adult/parental' mindset in here! It will be saying, "Don't be crazy". Ignore it! What does your 'child' want? When I was a kid, my grandmom would say, whenever I spoke of a career I might like, however unfeasible, "Why not? Someone's got to do it, so why not you?"

Do you just want a job where you can earn more money? Perhaps you aren't employed at the moment and just need a job... any job! In an ideal world, what is it that you'd really like to do? Perhaps a job isn't what you want at all, or things are perfect as they are? Write it down.

Finances: personally, I don't like money very much, but unfortunately in the world we live in it's essential for survival and to realize our dreams and ambitions. If your finances are a mess, then the task is to make them right. This often takes time and is the main thing that can hold back some of the more ambitious plans for changing our lives for the better. During the Step 1 exercise, you should have gotten a good idea of the current state of your finances. This is central to what you can realistically achieve in the short term to reach your goals. The most important thing is to acknowledge the problem. If you haven't done so already, speak with your creditors and get some kind of realistic re-payment plan in place. In the first instance, your goal needs to be financial stabilization at an amount you can realistically afford. Seek advice from a consumer debt organization if necessary; look into whether it's worth going down the debt management plan path. If poor finances are not an issue for you, then great! You will have more freedom right now to move towards your goals for better QOL.

For those of us who do have financial issues, there's still a lot we can do at little or no cost. If financial issues are pinning you down, a good antidote is not to dwell so much on what you haven't got, but what you have got. This, for me, is where the true power of writing regular gratitude lists is apparent.

...and finally

The tools I have described and the Method of how to use them are just the start. Building a more resilient sense of self, of emotional independence isn't something we do once and then are done with it. It's an ongoing process and what we have established can quickly fall apart if we neglect it – no, let me correct that: if we neglect ourselves. The moment we allow someone else to take priority, to occupy the top of the pyramid (as described in Chapter 6), we are losing ourselves again in someone else.

If you recognized 'The Cycle' (as described in Chapter 1) at work within yourself, then you are in a very strong position to interrupt it using the tools outlined in this short book.

8: COMING OUT OF CHRYSALIS

I shall spare you the clichéd butterfly-emerging-from-the-chrysalis metaphors. My use of the term chrysalis has more to do with my conveying the need to go into a protected place within ourselves, whilst we heal and create the right internal environment for emotional change. It's not anything to do with any eventual rebirth, turning into something beautiful. Besides I think I may have been pushing it a bit with the little girl and snowman analogy in Part One.

The lesson we can take however from the chrysalis idea is that change can take time. The natural process of grieving, for example, can't be sped up to an acceptable conclusion until we have processed grief. I'm saying that the same is true of the broken heart. It will take time to heal. Like any wound, it is best to stop the bleeding, to cover and protect it in the early stages of healing. The time this takes will vary from person to person. We can take action to aid healing, but we cannot avoid the process of healing itself, which can be painful. Of course you know that already because you have chosen to read this book. Your heart will mend, but no book, in itself, is going to do that for you. You can try and avoid emotional pain (withdrawal), but in doing so you delay healing. Accepting you are going to hurt is part of the process. It's a choice for us alone as to how we manage the pain and how long, to a large extent, we hold onto it.

Being in chrysalis isn't a state that should be prolonged beyond its usefulness. Avoiding a person, their social media profiles, and not communicating by any other means (if possible) is helpful in the short-term, but it's a temporary state that we allow for ourselves. It isn't a place in which to hide indefinitely. It's a tool we use whilst we go through withdrawal. You will know when the time is right to come out of chrysalis.

Almost shamefully, I've written of 'mechanics' in relation to a broken heart. On first appraisal this seems brutal. We aren't 'human doings', we are 'human beings' with feelings, not robots to be fixed with the right tools. We experience (among other emotions) love and joy, anger and loss. We are so much more than 'the cycle' outlined in this book, and the tools herein described. I categorically acknowledge this. Maybe it's a rough-around-the-edges explanation and way of suggesting how to manage the pain of love lost, but it tells us something more, beyond the semantics of language. It shows that we human beings can work things out, even if we have to apply crude concepts, in the most simplistic of ways to understand and achieve this.

Sometimes, a person we have loved, whom we still love, will occupy a space in our heart for a very long time, maybe until the day we die, or, who knows, beyond even? No-one else will ever take that place. It belongs to them and resides within us. The love we have to give may be infinite, and the heart is a very big place. Although no-one will occupy the already taken place in our heart, there is always room to love again when the time is right for us.

Some final words of caution about emotional independence. Whilst we can benefit from having a more robust sense of self and ability to meet our own needs, it doesn't mean we become one of the emotionally unavailable people mentioned more than occasionally in this book. Try not to slam the door of your heart shut forever. In all probability you will love again, and can take what you have learned from this painful experience and use it positively. May you be open to love.

When a relationship ends, when someone whom we love exits our life, the pain we experience is beyond mere Oxford English Dictionary definitions. It can feel as if our world has come to an end. I know; I've felt like this too. Yet, in time, and in gentle, reflective retrospect, I've also seen that a broken heart was the best gift I could ever have been given.

ABOUT THE AUTHOR

Paul Thorn is the author of five books and has been a regular self-help contributor to a variety of internationally published health and lifestyle publications for over two decades. In 2014 he was a finalist for Stonewall's Journalist of the Year.

He lives in Hove, England.

You can find out more about Paul and his work at www.e-m-press.com or follow him on Twitter @Paul_Thorn

Printed in Poland
by Amazon Fulfillment
Poland Sp. z o.o., Wrocław

50777235R00078